# Frames of Silence

for Russell Thornton

*unlike writing, life never finishes*
— Robert Lowell

# Frames of Silence

Allan Brown

Seraphim Editions

The publisher gratefully acknowledges the financial assistance of the Canada Council for the Arts.

 The Canada Council for the Arts
Le Conseil des Arts du Canada

Published in 2005 by
Seraphim Editions
238 Emerald St. N.
Hamilton, ON
Canada L8L 5K8

**Library and Archives Canada Cataloguing in Publication**

Brown, Allan, 1934–
Frames of silence / Allan Brown.

Poems.
ISBN 0-9734588-3-6

I. Title.

PS8553.R6848F73 2005     C811'.54          C2005-900913-6

Editor: A.F. Moritz
Cover photo: David Molyneaux
Design: Perkolator {Kommunikation}

Printed and bound in Canada

# Contents

# The Almond Tree

*The Imaginative Image returns by the seed*
*of Contemplative Thought*

– Blake

And the day returning,
the gone and day again
as such a tree remembered
staggers into this one
particular shape of:

How
my fragments swirl between
the globing places of the fog,
or slow come token of
forgetting, gentle as a hand
lifts seeds of the saying
rain; and dim as an egg
I mazing through
the long urge and cluster
of here the bright Pleiades
as small as air:

Stirs
in its sleeping how again
to flex the ratio
of each enbriefed
the countings from
our little death; and
alternate images
modify and fall between
that dream and the waking
known, if only knowing
is this mutant search
in the spongy day as
some this my strange return
is shaping a measure
of night and memory

(What
do you see?) if one again
to hold for that minute

the sound known now
in each tense identity
beyond the sweating tree
recovered,
and the cautious nerve
in the middle of snow
and almost winter is done.

⌒

Encumbering, a once shell
set at the ear
of my silly naked child
(the scrunch of fish bones,
the scatter of flax)
crisping to that pattern
of sand wealth and gull flight,
whisper-me, breed then (even
in creaking this stumbled place)
until again the strange
remembered day for-
given enters fir-wet
my having, but

                    is only
cicada secret lisps
me how is returned
to accomplish our purpose.

Or maybe no more than
the uncertainty of dust
in sunlight or
greyly the kept stone,
the pause between bell strokes,
the slow folding of wet grass;
or how the memory
of the golden dancers

who have become again
a fist of alephs
waiting name in name;
and now more quietly
they are taken them, passive,
dulcet, homely as bees,
as long the changing river
into each their tokening.

Once more
the indifferent flower to
image and claim recovered
in-where the shaking fog
until my mind become
its own encounter,
mirror and mime
in whose quick stone there
are no recognitions.

To wait, be, walk my gatherings
how is discernible
a frame of silence
where that vital motion
stirs elusively; the burning
shadow of the rain.

The almond flowering
in a forgotten night
unexpectedly,
the ghost and pattern
of, returns to inform
my wove involving, each
the slipping memories
with simple fire that,
single, fuses here

the inbreathing, holy night
to whatever gained
this mode be:

       What
do you see?
A flight of wild ducks
over the river; whether
my apriled knowing shapes
as well as these, the memoried,
felt weight of them at least,
and that recovery between
the alien awakening
of air and air, and
each my identities
in a long night are one
and interchanging.

These rise to my calling as
fingers flex them broody
as the lights of yeast
dividing, what time haply
the promise of how
that frugal opening
detains 'em soft and soft, and
the winnowed-of spirit wakes
between my shadows moving,
dark and dark it, to touch
the passing of what is
and is to be; and in
a hand's breath determining
that forgotten night if once
and yes to hold once ever
the single now and fond
articulation of
my changing death
into the waited fog.

# Nocturne Sequence

*In a dark time the eye begins to see*
— Roethke

## Vespers

*for H. A. Williams*


The shaking here, distorted mass
of the late garden fills slowly,
as a cluster of Japanese
lanterns crisply appearing and
my eyes re-focus, accepting
the edges of the night.

                    A touch
redeems, calls without naming, as
the body its own truth darkly
authenticates image and claim.

All knowing's such a mystery
perhaps, a losing to find, if
wholly the unsuspecting dream
where is a vein for silver (or
even here a gaining chance) or
where the unended day renews.


## II


The long orange thrust of late iris
in the quiet garden; the clouds fold,
the air is heavy with heat and slow
entrance of another evening and
the particles of flower, cloud, air
gathered now into the fallen day.

My words, they, dumb with sorrow, clumsy,
half-dreaming, speckled with insects and
the stupid, long-encroaching night is
almost come; the angel with dark wings
mute flutters.

        I heave into the air
one hour again or day and wait
in my remembered place of being
till the interchange of cloud foam-white,
incurious, in his motion stays
my apprehension of how it, yes,
whose spectre waiting in this evening
of variations without a theme.


## III


The changes of darkness;
                              but
the wave bears up within my veins
until, unwillingly, my bones
stutter again into motion and
I turn and pivot, a damned
dancer, remembering my change
but not what was changed when
May uttered itself into red
flower, red flower, and birds
swept, and the small ants
tumbled ferociously under the grass;

but not what the change becomes
when the raw earth breaks, and
the spider's web catches a whisper
of the wind, and the grey-lined snow
melts to a silent design of branches,
cardboard boxes, dogs' shit;

and the soft rain rumbles into
morning, and all the broken dream.

**IV**
"Kennst du das Land?"
*for Hugo Wolf*

Do you know it?
that country where his dream
is spoken in ever golden this now
(though no return from)
in-folding-flower time,

until the time of my
return: *kennst du es wohl?*
until the urge turns back
from oblivion in
red flower, red flower

under that quiet tree.
*Dahin:* when the wind cries,
in whatever silence
maintain the innocent
eye (beyond the hope of)

*wo die Zitronen blühn*
and the even pacing
white clouds indifferent
divide (where is my light?)
divide, where is my light?

## Ad Libitum

Extravasate,
the bitter fluid drawn
in shadow horns, they,
from the strange cave of morning;
and they are the substance
of that angel known here,
as my drunken fingers
tremble and clutch
the pages of another year and

extravagant
lights continue to play on
those rough, yellowing teeth; foam-
memory, the salty deposit
and ghost shape of slim beauty
in this place, in this dark
remembered like the thin line
delimiting madness.

The rough teeth flake and fall;
the dim edge of my vision
wavering into pale light,
plum light heavy with silence
before the first small birds –

                              here,
and the quick wind rising,
ruffles a dark wing
of this slipping cloud, and
the green light of morning
incorporate
falls slowly in shards of hope
through my waiting hand.

## VI

The heavy air releasing how
in slow dust of imagined turn
and completion of the one day
and year's end obscurely, who move
beyond my search and speaking; as
in the soft cavern of that face
and cloud-drift what memory stirs
the pure light of each year's start held
occasionally and without
pain;

      between the interchanging
darks of what discovery, shapes
heard in some half-awakening
when I do count the clock, until
the night comes, and I join the chance
and rich release of that chaos,
exchanging life for life;

            but day
now and I reach in my minute
for the smother of yr deep'd wings
to stay the sound of the long rain
falling, the untouchable night –

## VII
(Ars Poetica)

We come to our selving
accidentally, it seems;
and here an hour or so
as the decorous jaw line
of the long sky equally
in unexpected stars
thickens another name to be;

or into these own familiar
and mumbled shadows
shape 'em quietly till
certain a little and –
fingers of wood smoke, how
the fume reminds me as
each the edges opening, fickle
with meaning as a turned stone.

Oddly the interchange;
though I'm a sort
of nearer to it now,
that broken summer
and separating task;
uncertain again but
careful enough to the here,
as deer moving dusk-wise
out from an evening mist
to follow some further
my forms and symbols, where they lead.

# Winter Journey

*And whyte thinges wexen dimm and donne*
                                    – Chaucer

The almost smell of jonquils
in this year again dying
as each especial day's grace
forms, reforms in the place where
there are no words.

**I**

Unnameable, the bones of
morning are reflected here
marking what passage to our
alien country where are
no names or signs

to remember the effort
the hope and the end of hope;
the slow sun the marbled clouds
suspended in once again
this afternoon

and lucid minute of each
encounter with the angel
whose dark wings are centre and
limit of our appearing;
waiting silent

while the night fills, speech being
unnecessary at this time,
in this place where the lost day
is contained between soft hands
shaping shoulder

belly and thigh, and whose words
only of small hairs prickling
at tongue tip as the long cloud
forms, reforms in our ending
was it? or that other word
of day and day.

## II

The year ends: how quietly
the shoreline of this wrinkled
lake and the unforgiving
grey sky meet in the silence
of my lost years'

once glimpse of recovery,
of waters moving, sunplay;
and the small stones scatter in
luminous May change catching
that hope and what

hope surged to as my dark tree
imploding startles into
the strange lake, the memory
of lost days' shaping ana-
duomene

of life again in a year
and new beginning, water
pured; whether known or unknown
if once my sight renewing
pierces each lost

eye.
        But the edge of vision
is uncertain; and the wet
sky keeps only the shadow
that your holy minute made
till the day ends.

## III

The vague pulse of evening; and
parallels of reddened cloud
green or white and the faint sky
opens silently raging
beyond that deep

silence; something left, between
the mask of mediate thought
and the sweet mouth of the night
in bodiless interchange;
shapes flow, and how

one day after another
is endurable only
to find myself contained in
the lucid geometry
of life for life

exchanged at the mid point and
unfeeling centre of one
my chance to determine edge
and being here, spinning in
the small air till

I

crumble into another
day and the white moon bulges
pale as ice in this last sky
and dawn again

appearing in th'especial
green of madness
or remembered as what bird
song shaped in the long night's
awareness of your name un-

speakable if I must be
again as I have been, as
into the unknowing light

the choice of making casts
the half of one
                    /one
value into no values
determinable, inchoate,
unprayable

design;
          indifferent how
it is made some memory
and source of our encounter
in these bright stars;

but I don't know
who can hear them,
                        their laughter
and their soft voices because

their voices are repeating
night and night the night's end, as
into the blank and sullen
dawn I shriek with the laughter
of my mad birds

                    /as
I shriek with the laughter of
my mad birds into the blank
and sullen dawn.

## IV

I remember, when the night
softens and the opening
moonlight shapes a saraband
of your neck and endlessly
the dark rain falls

as a muscle in my foot
stiffens – how sweet the moonlight
sleeps upon this something or
other
      The wall heaves: and now
only somehow

to evade the dull clock face
before my delivery
from all these very quiet
people
      can be accomplished
again (don't move,

don't even scream) cautiously,
even though I realize
quite well just where I'm at, and
seemingly without much con-
cern
      tip

tip
tip
   my soft cat ears trembling
with subtly imagined sounds
as if I was afraid or
something
      or the other,
but I'm not; I know where they are;

they can't fool me; even now,
because I've been here before
tip-tip
          and found the way out;
then, relying

upon my tracker's instinct
which has never failed me yet,
with a long practiced furtive
skill I consult the compass
of my palm and

my slowly little fingers
contract, deploy like shrunk dew
about the silver winding
screw, hold
                and the ticking stops.
I knew it would.

Like it always did before.
All you have to do is wait.
Oddly enough, though, I seem
to have forgotten just what
it was entered

my skull in a crystal of
sweet dew when the light broke like
the hot dust of one August
day in particular where
our walk ended

behind a broken cedar,
grunting, sweating in the short
grass, breath with breath taken, as
our mouths echoed each spasm
till my bird dropped

squeaking out of her nest – tip
tip? twitter twit? or something
about an ending; I think
it was an ending; or what's
the other word?

I keep getting them mixed up.
Well, let's call it the ending
of each day unknowable
beyond the placeless to be
again one of

my darkness determining
once a way upon a time
how all word look and gesture
sung sweet in the evening when
the sun goes down.

Something again,
                    the contours
of life and only death merg-
ing candid and surprised to
praise in the holy silence
of the tumble

of your hair. Sunlight giggling
in the still pool: look, psyche,
here's a body come to grow
in the image of how this
your shining hair;

in whatever body now,
my love, whether this alien
dim night will end with your hand
gentle in my dream of dawn,
your quickening hair

is heavy in my hand and
I must draw from that darkness
only the stutter and turn
of each day's ever dying,
anticipate, remember –
well,
        once again.


## V


Quiet as the snow shifting
unexpectedly from dark
to light till I am mocked by
the echo of my own voice:
I clear my throat

and phlegm trickles like lava
through the inhabited streets
of my gregarious mouth
reflecting silver sponges
or snow droppings

dimly; meanwhile, unheeding,
nose sings a merie tune and
poem discusses itself
(for the most part, anyway)
in thirty-two syllables
and five lean lines.


## VI


How can I say to you, my
bird, when each moment of snow
play, the bright drift and tumble
describing alternate life
and life of you

in this deep quiet turning;
when the lean grey sky again
softens into evening and
the blue shadow of the tree
arches, quickens

my autumn memory like
the quarter moon emerging,
dividing as a small air
and shape, time reach together
their pause; little

bird, whose silence is the place
of my beginning, growth now
uncertain, tortile, pauses
because I have seen your breasts
swaying slowly

as you walk in delicate
snow play, and the moon returns
unexpectedly with what
challenge
          to consume my day
uncertain now;

until the single quiet
breath of each white thing
                         divides
and the long wind changes and
the clear water of that lake
reflects my dream where *blauen
licht die Fernen;*

but the shape of it again,
the day it returning in
natural perspective that
is and is not, resisting,
touching sunlight.

Their skin against my skin is
cold as iron, intricate
with leaf vein and melting scars
crinkle till *alle Sehnsucht*
*will nun träumen;*

but what self remaining then,
what one thing perceivable
as the irregular line
of consciousness scatters, fades
leaving the blank

memory of one growth known
in the sky and the cold lake
whose margin flutters against
my sweating bones, as the sky
shrinks to new day

and your silhouette dances
through each my howling night,
or single determining
doubled, glittering in planes
of ragged light;

and again the words of you
echo in this iron rain,
the extension and spirit
of my year, though start lost and
no ending till

my thin skull in frozen wings
of almost comprehended
pain echoes, echoes your word
and will that cannot, must be,
is, is not, is.

## VII

There is only one question
ever unspeakable, as
body gropes, all sentience
to the reasonless design
of one and one

in that place where each action
is recovered, the circle
of start and centre renewed
to determine action, urge
and consequence;

because love is action, not
beginning and goal only
but the sustaining body
of untouchable time – and
twenty years breaks

like strained threads, unbodies in
the yellow scream of jonquil
mirrored in now this dumb lake
till the drowned weed quickens in
my shaping hands – if light wakes
in the scatter

of small stones whose once pattern
repeats (each is the ghost of
a day or minute) the grace
of our passage, if the year
breathes again and

my slow flowers are released
like wrinkled fiddlehead ferns
swelling in warm water, if
each day ends – but *ohne Ruh,*
*und suche Ruh.*

## VIII

Now I lay me down to sleep
as gentle as a flower
whose petals are still dry it
seems
        and the chance of somewhere
a
  what did you say?

The light thickens.

My loosening tendrils suck
at these hard roots

as th'insurgent stem wiggles
before I wake up to re-
member a how tentative,

what did you say?

wait
     a little longer;
give me whatever you can;
I'll dream the rest of it out
until the dumb

the fruitful dark releases
into one sight and being
something of you
               remaining;

the pale,
       milk seeming
of your young breasts,
slurred r's under cloth;

words of the unpointed sky
rehearsing now each act in
virginal mensuration
and word of the dying year.

As everything fits into
place again,
    articulate,
under control;
and I am indifferent
as the cuckoo's

falling third placeless in what
afternoons of uncertain
horizon, as I swell once
now, if once only, moonhard
in pale morning.


**IX**


The muffled ice sinks in slow
chimes mourning the long year's death;
the brittle black tree shakes like
a hand into this silence;
*de profundis clamavi*
*ad te:* until

the upward striving blind quest
of the hooded pilgrim is
achieved, is consummated
finally in firmly your
coign of vantage;

in his mouth a coal of fire,
dissolving in heavenly
dew; but I am recusant;
my flaccid god lies unpropped
by any cross

because I have finally
come to the soft place of pain
and the bells have stopped ringing.
Oh, I wouldn't deny that
it was hard on

me to leave you, and I still
wonder how many graces
the new morning will reveal,
or whenever it was that
the slow grey drift

of cigarette ash speckled
unexpected age upon
my succulent dark root and
my leaves tremble like a cat –
just a minute –

I think I've said that somewhere
before
      I ramble;
it took a while to get here;
however, in

spite of my digressions I
hope that you will have noticed
that I do retain a lot
of my religious habit
and cast of mind

(not everything passes) and
I praise you now as then with
pious ejaculations.
I water my flowers; I
wait.
      The question

ever, the question remains;
because, no, there aren't any
words to ease the one burden,
powerless, without a name.
Well, I'm free now,

content to be alone with
the mark and sacrificial
sheet of my moist survival,
dripping into another
day and, day and

# Lunations

*A long days dying to augment our paine*
                                    – Milton

## The Clearing I

To follow the late sun
a little onward
into what place now
recognizable,
waiting to meet
the copper sunlight
over this round
of green ponds, the quiet
of crowded roots;
the soft entanglement
of bent cedars and
these scattered grasses pause,
wonder passing
in this clearing
into fear of place
and past again;
and how the limit
met, urging yet
my words to calculate
the undated year.

## Silences

Dumb with waiting,
uncertain in
or out of this place
whose slow shout breaks
between the shapes
of unrepeating
nights, expands to
once my imagined
vanity of seeing;
reach in the lost
and breathing darkness
how, or clutch once more
your lucent fragments
to retain that truth
who waits beyond
each new day; in
the heave of my blood
remembered, your
immaculate body
contains me without
effort; although
the atoms of my breath
remaining hold this long
and autumn trance to reach
an end of each the once day
in these elements
again to tell
the uncertain way
of my return
that is and gone
*Selah*

And the clearing night
like a soft wing
rises through here
my silences, re-
lieving the loose pain
and clamour of
what day my waking.

## Moon

Here she is again,
an old white woman
climbing slowly
the sky road. Her
rising is contained
in nearly the limits
of that forgotten
night.

    The while
her middle growth concludes
ambiguously, brightness
against brightness
in the loose, unpatterned
stars;

    and I can still remember, even if she doesn't, how we set out one morning earnest and early, she being about thirteen at the time, hornet-slim and tight as an apple; stalked the trail and our dreams out together till we stood again blinking through the good, the cool day.

# Enna

And freshly still the sight of her
shapes carefully that clear
and winter road;
my thick pulse catching
(what do you see?) hints,
scraps of the poppy-wet
incongruous field
of myth-darkened Enna
whose minute aligns
this uncertain body,
urging memory
into immediate form
to reach here if here only
a pause of why
the strange making.

Red clouds fail
before the taken dark;
no known place now,
guess or entrance
into whatever day,
until the long fingers
of this tree pierce
my door like a grave
and I wake I see
the altering moon
suspended over
the extended fibres
of once that clearing,
the intricate
layers of cedar
almost visible
in the little dirt,

almost remembering
some last dry seeds
of summer, luminous
ejaculate
rising through the warm-
made-immaculate sea
to wonder again
the gain or loss of:

further now into
her placeless story
to reach a close
of that curious search
for the day's end
and once limit. It
will not be long
till her dying.

The brightness dims;
the ring shakes softly
into deeper night;
the nimbus clears.

## Madonna Cloaca

The idiot and echo
of that moon, now only
the waiting remains,
forgotten things;
as awkwardly
your bended light
in this clear morning
of unworded time
renews my reach
for each beginning
claimed, how the one
light of you suspends
my once moment till
(*Selah*)

        my changing
will becomes shadow
and profile to your
unconsummated
erotic pilgrimage
through yesterday's
labyrinth of public
lavatories and
enter again
our dreaming, caught
in each my frenzies now,
shape in that blankness
what minutes
I wake each day,
and how the prism
of your name breaks until
the limit met, urging
still the one absurd
image and dark moon
of our memory

into silence;
and only this to end
my computation:

                     how
my words again in
wonder rising
each completed night,
uncertain as
our moving, yet the long
inconsequence and tale
of how these years, in
the cool the clear dawn
almost appearing.

## The Clearing II

Quiet and
the lean moon pauses,
poised dimly in
these white autumn fields
to fill the breath
and blood of memory
with yet some fertile chance
or change, reflecting
what uncertainty
remains; the place between
water and rock where
the light gleams, the word
I look for, some token of
again our passage.

                Wait
a minute longer in now
this open space until
each ghost returns, no
matter how the call
or long completion
of here the slow walking.

## The Cave

Remembered, yet
I do not understand
how dust again and
startled these sleepers
of yesterday's seeming
loss now caught in
the atoms of my breath;
though I have seen
her lean immediate move
contain the changing space
of each excluding day.

And returning
through the copper branches
of our hidden place,
until my waiting
falters at the rough edge
unexpectedly,
consuming your white
flower and all lost time;
erects and renews
our wasted direction
into whatever
movement now, un-
worded once chance
of reach and limit
meeting to
begin again.

                    Here
is the smeared light
weightless, quiet, renews
the stations of slowly
that old white fool.
There are tenders

of sense and grace held
in this cautious place,
unknowable
entrance to alone
the hollow dark.

My parts dilate
like separating leaves
in a slow fever; fingers
suck bubbling air of
uncontrollable cold
fire; my chest fills
with straining yeasts,
clots of precise death.
I taste my pulse
that winks in pain;
my branches splinter
my huge eye.

## Midsummer

The loosening stars
divide me, merging
these scattered memories
like interchanging
day and day of mid-
summer uncertainly
aware, subside
to the mulch of whose
slim bones crackling in
ever this place where
the sweating Archer
rested; and both
content now to wait
through the heather-red
passing of the stupid
moon
       *Selah*

The sound of bees
centers my wonder;
here is the lost
thing almost plain;
I hear your voice
between the half wind
rising, what pause?

And how the vacant
green and soft grey
fingers of the leaves
caress my throat,
repeat our small veins
image and gain;
as all left particles
of once our effortless
contention beyond

each new margin tensed,
resilient as sand
to a slow wave's breaking
in endless this scatter, year
and days of:

      who?
I raise my head
to the forgotten call

what ghost is this?

## Kommos

What was it then,
the once articulated
recompense or sight
again, the echo
of delight caught
in this hollow place
whose pause consumes
the nodes of my year,
beginning and beginning
to trace the poppy frame
of memory
uncertainty and breath,
absorbs the scintillae
of pushed eyeballs till
their irrelevant seed
spills into the night.

Her sprawling growth
elusively is met
with a kind of comfort
in the last portions
of these attenuated
hours and each again
borrows the reach
and relaxing of new
returns; and a little
clearer as I turn once
more exchanging day
for day now, writing
in the early morning
of nearly forgotten
agitations, mocked
by the snubface moon;

who else will sing
berceuse for you?
                    be grateful.

# A Gift of the Earth

*The words that mean a gift of the earth*
                   – Tom Wayman

# I

His father's a king, King Ban
of Benwick – or so he told me
one day – I don't know for sure,
because we'd always called him
du Lac (or Dulac) and not
Benwick; still, I don't suppose
it really matters.

What does, certainly, is that he
was, well, the best there was;
best at everything – riding,
the jousting, fighting, singing (a kind
of high baritone), courtesy – saying
the right thing at the right time,
being modest and so on – and,
as everyone knows, he was in love
with Guinevere, Arthur's wife, though
that isn't important here – at least
I don't think it is.

                    He
(Launcelot, I mean) was always there
when you needed him, sometimes
it might be even before you knew
that you needed him, ready
for a fight (of course) or
a joke or a quiet, really
serious talk, before, after
or even during the drinking –
it didn't seem to matter much
to him – and so it was only
natural, only to be expected
that when the Grailing, as
they called it in the song –
the Grail quest, you know – when

it finally did begin, that
old Launcelot (he was getting on
at the time) would step forward –
quietly though, almost as if
everyone weren't looking at him.

We all went, it was the thing
to do; and most of them
looked determined enough – talked
enough, at least, about the work.
Not, mind you, that very many
of them would have much of a chance
at it – I certainly didn't,
on grounds of basic chastity
(thought and deed) alone, never mind
the holiness aspect; but Launce said
"Never mind" – I hadn't even asked him –
"Never mind what *they* think
they're going to do," and I understood
exactly what he meant, "Let's start
early tomorrow." Which was very nice
of him, as usual; so we did.

## II

And I made it about
as far as –
                   well, I used to say
about as far as
the first damosel at
the second pit-stop (ha, ha)
but, strictly speaking, that's not true;
it always got a laugh, though
(almost always) and –

The truth is, I don't know
what happened, never did – it wasn't

a blackout, not in the ordinary sense
of the word – at least, not like anything
I'd ever experienced before, and
the damosel part wasn't even
half a joke any more.

                        "There
they go," he said and laughed,
telling me again what had happened
as if I hadn't heard it all –
how they went on, here and there,
passing him with "the relentless
competence of telephone
repairmen" is the way
he put it, I think.

It was on the last evening
we spent together, which – as
I said – I don't remember
very well – though in fact
we eventually passed
most of them – or so I learned
later, when I had the chance
to look into things again
back in Logres.

                    There were always
reports coming in about who
was where, when, and had done
or hadn't done what – a sort
of running score being kept
that began as fun (bitching,
really) but went on
all the time, it seemed, not
malicious, just a way
of knowing without asking
or being asked, where
we all were and who
had managed to return.

## III

So, what happened? he didn't get it
(Galahad did, eventually) but
just why I don't understand.

He goes there – actually got there
and came back, the old Launce,
that serious, sort of quizzical
look on his face, hands still dirty,
sort of whispering in that
high voice for so big a man,
tired, of course, very tired; and
it took quite a while for him
even to say any more
about it than ask after King Pel,
Gareth, Kay, some of the others –
Arthur himself it was
brought him up to date, and the Queen
standing close, washing his arms
down, helping to clean his beard.

He didn't say much to them,
nothing else really that
he didn't repeat to me
and anyone else who asked –
though not very many did,
or only for the chance to add
a few more details to prove
they'd seen some of the things too.

He didn't know what it was,
or couldn't ask, or something
just about as stupid. I mean,
we all knew what it was,
didn't we? it's what
we'd been told or asked or
whatever to find and bring
back again – and he found it,

I know he did, even though
he wouldn't say so, wouldn't
tell them – he never really
told anyone anything,
if it came to that, nothing
you could make any sense of;
and he's getting worse these days,
now that his son has come and gone
away and rumours of all
the old troubles again and
Arthur getting gloomier
every day –

        All right,
I understand, sort of, what
this kind of adventure is
and why it's so different
from all those others, but
did you have to go so far
just to prove there's always
some other kind of failure?

# La Corona: A Marian Novena

*I synge of a mayden*
*That is makeles*
– medieval lyric

## Stabat Mater

How many times before
did she come to this never
before seen place, quietly
assuming the grace and station
of him, into the grave
remembered music
that moved simply and
with pure seeming a once
similitude of God.

And now you wait again,
mother, daughter, child:
the soft triangle
of your face almost
startling once more
into brown-eyed brat
all flutter and joy
as the sky brightened
after rain and you saw
in that moment
somewhere a gesture
of infinite forgiveness.

## Stella Matutina

At lake-edge of you
the awareness
of still that solemn
joy receives word
and salutation;

patient until
the illumination
and peace of uncertain
happiness moves in
the portions of the waves;

and your waiting here
enacted like
the first sight, the prime
of dandelion
in the morning grass.

## Nazareth I

*And in the sixth month the angel Gabriel was sent from God, unto a*
*city of Galilee, named Nazareth.*

Meeting the numinous, once the thing happens, is really quite
simple. It's there, if it is, and that's about all there is to it. The
practical, logical problems of such a situation are far more
difficult to accept and deal with. After all, it isn't so hard now to
envisage a thirteen or fourteen-year old, say, who knows enough
about Satan, his works and all his allurements to renounce them;
probably it never was. They are, after all, collected, general
notions and can be dealt with in a general manner, by taking a
certain simple or relatively uncluttered position of argument,
expectation, whatever.

But this was a particular, a very particular thing; and, of course,
the common sense of a young Jewish girl was well enough
developed (had to be) to question the statement, let alone the
enormous promise made to her. The wonder is that she had the
temerity actually to speak the words – or so it seems from this
point in time. Nonetheless, she did; and, most significantly,
facing such an impossible proposition, did in fact face it, and
made the utterly impossible possible just by saying yes.

## Pray for Us Now

Into your stillness
the splendour of his dew
certain in the morning
splashes freely
before the fear of yet
that morning repeating
till your almost tears,
Mother of Joy,
in the soft cadence
of each new morning's
fear and dignity
exposed

      Absorbing
the fret and the water,
the waste of his day
and first awakening.

Until
our separating flames
ascending sear
the casual insignias
of gull-flight between
the changing wind as past
present and future from
that breaking night

contain, sustain:

Blessed among women,
*pray for us poor sinners*

## The Vigil

She is the patience
and faith of a peasant
generation centred
in this place, this now
of eternity.

Her waiting shoulders
are pliant with how
the soft and shaking night
contains her neat hair
flowing darker
into the darkness.

Even this will end;
and a small bird
glitters, rising into
the graceful encounter
of each the new dawn.

## Advent

It's getting harder to remember now, not just when things
happened and what they were – in any detail, I mean – but who
it was they happened to; everything seems to shift and change
so much. Yet I can still hear the voice whenever I wonder and
ask; and it's still the same, certain and clear, the silence after
speech, before the last dawn that seemed little different from a
hundred or so others, how

>           (arriving at last
>           in the partly remembered
>           place, and the sun behind
>           them, struggling into
>           their shadows, breathe
>           and breathe again;
>
>                       though
>           it tarry, yet it will come)

each discovery empties into only one image now, beyond the
edge of that truth, relieving the pressure of again those words
and the sky all full of the otherness.

## The Flight into Egypt

They travelled into
the odour of the night,
their footsteps echoing
the angel's voice;

their dread behind, that death
still somehow to come;
the clear way persisting
in a faint trickle
of the dim path,
illuminated
by a fragment
of the slim moon only
in deepening cloud;

yet her faith like soft eyes
in fear and wonder
equally contained
as that night ended;

timorous even
at the child's quick laughter
as a myrrh tree made
a funny face at him
in the early dawn.

## Nazareth II

Almost able at times
to enter again
the before silence
of the angel's bright words;

her eyes are blurred
with that deep music
ever, but never
known, the thrust of him,
the five petals
of (yes) yet to come
his precious flower;

but each day begins
again, and
she is able
almost to forget
the way he will walk;

she waits and watches
the young boy grow.

## Not Yet

No return, no
new again gaining
of that fragrant place
(even before these days
are gathered, swollen,
broken in the big sky,
inscribe it on tablets
to be easily read)
between the deep wind
whose hidden hold
equally ever
untouchable met
(wait, it will come)

Not yet, but this
always – the bearing
memory of once
in the sunlight,
his frown and uncertain
crown tumbling into
laughter;

       my bairn,
my blithe one.

# Meeting at Deventer

*A man goes far to find out what he is*
                                    – Roethke

His arrival was probably
unexpected, the time of it
unknown anyway, in
a strange city and having
travelled about two or three
days from Kempen, limited
to the hours (roughly speaking)
of prime to vespers, tented
in his darkness, between
the river's turning, then
to be accommodated
in this place for a certain
time; re-

      placing as
again the terms of it,
the half-remembered story
alternate now for then,
then for now only, lighted
indiscriminately here
and there to a pause between
the windings of this calm
warm night, in Kingston
near the end of May
(and the twelve-year-old
Thomas Haemerken walks
a bit faster through the streets,
knocks and enters).

      Quiet again,
and still the truth,
the lie of it remaining
inwardly (for both of us
who endure even in this
unlikely collocation
our strangely wondering
dialectic) as a few

words recollected and
somehow contained even
if not yet understood
(although in this, the waiting,
it is still like any other
experience)

       becoming
into this change more quickly
aware now of our casual,
uncertain meeting, as
the various determined pulse
of each my spasms of themselves
unspeakable crumble
into the clotted, the
bitter dust of Golgotha
that is
       no, more than that.

However completed, the end
itself is our story,
incomprehensible, sufficient,
marrowing between
His bones; the agon deeply
falling in swell and skin
to the one gaining place,
understood no more than
a perfected, only
exclusion of any movement
here, one-colour-bit chances
of memory, or this pain
that I may conveniently
find less and less difficult
to realize or even distinguish
in sharp and immediate
contours –
       the sound between

my breath and always just
slightly ahead and feeling
toward whatever equal
ending or pause there
may be to show the way
of it more clearly, looking
both ways, up, down, before
and after jumping;

               whether
or not each making renews,
the site at least has become
nearly intelligible
now, and waiting again
each day to heal with Amen
the changes of something
almost about to be.

And always another place
and a time, the bits of one
anyway, orts and fragments
becoming clear enough
to wait with whatever sort
of patience faith is, until
we discover both ourselves'
and one another's newly
one substance in here
the reconstruction
of that Agony which is
enough and more, more or less
following the work plan
it could be called or set
of guides, a few lines left
husky with fear

            (and again
the young man from Kempen

walking now a little
quicker than his fear into
the certain streets)

                          as
the whine of a car bends,
framing the urge of what
or who it was contained
our meeting there;

                          spastic
fragments of conversation
unequally suspend
the heavy air *in cruce*
*pro homine,* till slowly
our quiet resettles line
against line, like the thick
grey walls of that house
in Deventer, still crisply
apparent though somehow
difficult to remember
with any precision and
much smaller than expected.

# Moss-Wind

*from the north the moss-wind blows*
　　　　　　　　　　　　　　　– Melville

## Étude for St. Francis

A fist of berries
on the mountain ash
and nothing stranger than
a leafy something in the water,
or uneasy a bit
the waited compassing,
if here or t'other
and no nearer than needful.

(The Teachers say that *ruah gedola*,
the "largish winds" of Job and Jonah, can
be limited – quite human, really – in
applications, though infinite in cause.)

                    And then
another, pace and pace
my creaking eidolon, who
through that fear of clouds;
until by losing, found,
and by unknowing, known.

# I

The plummet settled half a throw
and quietly, the cracks and code
together come.

        Flutters the each
bland seed too long a waiting,
maybe, how to bulge the warm
and awful giving this; paused
delicate to enter, if
the blithe of me
a wobble out from such play
cautious to the season
weighing. Well. Taken the gate
re-sounds, and marrow is the way
to freeing.

# II

        Here the jantees
plump as any's kisses, scatter
*poco a poco* 'cross the thwack
of a green new'd dawning; and
neither closer nor beyond
the prophet's grave and under-
taking, gains of a saying
what these measures yet, into
lightened their westering where to
place and place; the voyage
continues.

## III

       The night wind rises.
Is this a further way to live?
My silver trims a warm breath
now, the candles remaining,
and they are still as any bone.
A little loving would be
easier to pause than this,
I kinda think.

       Shapes
and the somewheres out
of each expected turns
'em back to savour again.
The growing's quirky. Even
the least of patterns leaves
me rubbled a softer tread.
But wonder does as wonder is
(the lighted minutes changing,
obscure and most fitfully)
and all these parted echoes hold.

## IV

Here is a green thing suddenly
(as near to the body
as shifty a truth can come)
leads thus its curious edge
outing that three-day wander
a bright of the waitful,
pale and necessary air.

And then the dove did, and
God-wording whole things never
a truth or not, indeed;
but climbed him back the how
each hair shaken, numbered, comes
a kind of satisfaction
only. Themes, if new-a-day
grown? the wayward pulse
continuing these minutes all,
and brach-me bellowing yet.

**V**

*And then another. Nearly*
*did me too, the bugger.*

             Splits
the hollow each dark I do,
points me so to the coasting plain.
The blue man in 's scraggy coat,
he gestured me. We heaped a bunch
for burning, though I didn't think
there would be time enough to pass
a chunk of him. I didn't think
I was his memory too.

*I'm getting thinner. Who's*
*for dinner? Mouse knows*
*the answer to that: go dance*
*on your toes.*

           This my centre,
still a much bendable thing:
but which next, Lord, my turning?
What taking through the neared dark
a patch and plug for Cerberus?
or how the way declines, or
where the voyage rarely.

              One
and one my creaking birds
are subtle from their crannies,
peak 'em to whatever a day
more ready than ever the pouch
and pokey did; and shape
and not, my gullet bending
here an only spitful.

## VI

The fire is curious how
my glib and dusty rises – stuff
without stamen. I can do
another sorted thing – finds
me a bull for stoking, laying
greeney and grown to market
together; keep at it too;
not narry the first fizzle
in a chance maybe, but
I'm stealthy rounding with
my dexter sticks, pull 'em each
without a knuckle napping;
and here I'm laying again;

                      keep
certain at least the ashes
cleared away, ding out
the unflammable bits
and tender all t' others only
a little worse in the wet.

Spindle through, the downtime gnats
remember and a thing is done,
is cared and who in the catch
these wordings a-shuffled
be sorted yet; the nether turns,
the newly burns, and resheph
now I follow a half-me upward;
bunching, touched, and droop again
skin-weary, in a wobble come
to briefly this held content.

## VII

In the deep nook, safely.

We're left to a cold bed,
you and I, some awkward floating
yet before the silly dawn,
and least unprofitable
nears that grounding, mortal wind
a flat to say. There
is not a meeting to be
reckoned for us in or out
of taken's this time *pro* ...
*ora* ...

     and I think the fire
is white now, dry and mooney
and very near; but not
him a new – do you see?
to whatsome entering; but
one in's truckle bed alone
remembers and the rest
itself no longer limber
to.

  Nor tells the bone either,
of how those names were reckoned,
each to come my knowing day
and day;

     or if she once
(who limned my gatherings)
in dipped the neither ashes
from this alien lake-to makes
a most of understanding.

## VIII

Between their breathings
wait. It is the night wind
heard, loon-heavy, marks
another place than this, I think,
bare to the keepings of
Elijah's ghost, that raven man
deserted and repairing
hopes him a little and then
a little more.

                    – Tried forty,
or fifty paces, was it?
careful in the mouth, and
almost made it back again;
too many stones, though; noisy.

What kind of map is this?
The water's so deep my ankles
are getting rusty. A bit
of blood should see me
together. I'll nap when nearer
to the running place. This death
will fit quite nicely, I do
believe, and half a leg's better
than none. I'd shake a wing too,
if I had one.

                *Anything*
*fills the come-to, with a bit*
*of practice: and do we ever*
*practice anything else?*

## IX

But every new that solemn time
now's back-winding? something like,
it seems. A touch surprises.
How very loose each parting is;
a dottle left burns right a way,
and spirits, they say, must live
in the places they lived before,
same streets and houses? I
gibber a bit now, learning
by rote each my degrees,
and verge me careful if I count
through any the ways them how
the lean mouth deemed (is
here and clearly), hold yet
half the linden back; and slouch
me to the waiting mutt a jerk
and jiggle only.

*(Word stuff*
*that, and dread the echoes,*
*gaming for once a candle*
*was, and who the worm to be.)*

# X

No bloody way. A softly word
will do. The piece of him.
Whether the big wind ruffles,
or who-we only that lonesome
whistle till all the crows
come home.

    I act and patient me
a hunger more to tracing, as
my once that start *in selva*
to the certain samed-of close;

the foggy shape, the shudder heard,
the elf and trickle beckoning
some further a day; and 'ware
the knowing obscurely that God
who is found in and through
every life is found in
and through every death also.

And if the voyage yarely ends?
Signs and seasons. A thin smoke clears.

# Antics Against the Long Night

*i who am but imperfect in my fear*
– e.e. cummings

## The Number of the Beast

Word is a wanderer
delicate to hear
or there what calling
not quite recognizable,
because the poem's always
something other; how
each new mageing
in my awkward eyes that form
and forming once before
a time the shaqed saw me
and I could not speak;

if only a crinkling of
the long night wondered
if what's true is what's left over and
what we see made possible
by what we do not; as the skin
that knows its selvings, part by part,
by what presses upon it; or
the stones of this bridge
set each against the other, as
say:

those slow green filaments of "Driftwood
and seaweed floating in the water
and shore birds flying overhead" until
your paths cross and you've been
going west and then you're going south
without changing direction.

                              (Sometimes
it takes a while to get your shadow on
just right.)

*He'd tried that once, captured and then let slip*
*a twisty lotan to his growing and*
*summer a way as near to knowing as*

*any if this smell with its wetness is*
*the drenching in the lilac by means of*
*the lilac.*

       A nudge and again
the shifty edges
further a turn or two
whose saying still within
the sound of this water,
crisply rumorous, crowing
a careful and warm-handed count
of now my 20,000 days of June
before the thick rush flushed upon
a coast-not-understood;

or could remember anything more
than when this sinister giggle
a step and steps on
the early water moving,
and the several fingers
who rise and comprise me,
and half a step's outward
till what is left of my head
at the first touch of

            (more or less)
the heavied peony loosens, scatters,
white stuff on the grass; but
nothing else, no pathetic fallacy here it's just
a busted flower isn't it?

       So
why don't I change colour when it rains?

## A Sinne of Feare

In the dream you are trying
to "See more deeply" – Thoreau's dictum.
(Absorb me, old furrow.) Some parts
of seeing are surface always.
Those bubbles in the ice are – bubbles?
something more? Yes and no.

Are parts (again) of the ice;
or maims, perhaps, of what
is left, till an art maybe
not as long as itself; enough,
though incomplete.

           "The pen,"
intones the Stroller rather pompously,
"is perfected by its drawing."

[follow this statement with a <less than> or
<nothingness> image, as "I have a sinne of feare"
(cf. "on the shore")]

Always lose something for luck.

Item: the smell of wet lilac
till whatever ending;
or was that just another edging
after all, if one inword is such or
less than another.

The distinctions of what
is real and what is something else
apparently

     *I was talking to Allan*
*the other day and he said like he saw*
*the Sleeping Beauty – you know, that profile*

*the mountains make – knees and boobs and her brow*
*and hair flowing back – and she just got up*
*and walked down through the North Shore,*
*crunching all the houses and everything –*
*I didn't believe it but*

*pace* the Port-Royaliste,
it is not the infinite but
the all too precisely finite spaces
*m'effraie.*

                As:
the repetition
but not quite repetition
of these images because
there are no metaphors for death:
itself its acting (if thus,
then so); not the unknown
but the known puzzles.

And I can blow or stay
any thing that I walk to; after all,
it is my dream.

*He nods in passing to his enemy's shadow,*
*misses; observes a falling leaf; drops*
*another pebble and keeps on going*
*as the sky flutters and fails.*

## Which I Is I?

*And half a skip more from puddle to puddle*
*between the early and the late rains dripping.*

My new lover,
whose name is the same as mine,
is listening to
the water the rocks
the sound of water on rocks.

*These particles of quartz-fret and the eyes*
*of Jonathan Swift bulging with so great*
*a pain he tries to tear them out by twos*
*and twos, or splinter the mind exhaling,*
*thus:*

    am I incoherent? very
well then, I am incoherent.
I am loose, I contain losings.

I will show you Allan
speaking and what Allan says; but
recognize please that he
is not contained in nor
the content of this saying;
neither what I am, but what when
this is written I will
have been

      (or something like) though
I'll have to take the rest
of my skin off for that.

Or that place sometimes in a poem
when the almost balance, a couple
of bits askew, but the slant of it

as – "Hi there! d'you still remember
me?" – slinks a step closer,
the little toes stretching till
cannot be seen much longer between
the leaf, the shadow on the leaf

                                Or
maybe the old farter simply ran out
of words;

          but not quite
repeating the bits and pits
(or maybe that man
going mad in that field
painting his crows) because
there's nothing, or anyway
not much else other than

                        "You just
don't get it," she snickers, "do you?"

Or was it the other why?

## L'Invitation au voyage

*One any note implies a measuring*
*of silence through the boney night, contracts*
*in scatters of skin-bright; how*
*each particular of rhododactulos*
*eos on the early water moving.*

"The light, contained, quickens."

Every person, my enemy murmurs,
will encounter the end of time
once. So each life just
long enough, and her version of the story
equally, say,
if Cleopatra's clit
had been a finger's print shorter,
the history of the world.

As in the perfect dictionary,
for instance, where every word
is defined in terms of
every other –

       or maybe
even a white page so I could look
more like Marcel Marceau
who says things quietly.

        ↜

The poet and his son
are traveling north by west,
establishing the lines and pleasant places
carefully each day
recorded, but not my birthday
or deathway recorded.

They get their supplies, and out
on the Monday morning; a day
and approaching Rogue River, but
they have not seen Rocky Point and
encounter some curious seemings:

like the place
in his face that separates
Greco and Crazy Harry
from Stanley Cooperman; and
who's sorrow now if
Pat Lowther's lightly dried blood
makes briefly an appearance
on the smothering beach?

They float clear again as
plain's for sailing; and Eric
Ivan Berg is bright on the grass
in his smear of resin
(whose more's the less of that);
until they can see
so quietly you could hear a pin
draw interesting lines
suggesting bone to its home.

The poet and his son consider
these matters for a while
and a couple of years;
they return south eastly
and they don't see me either
or smell me other
than mostly the porous
and filling pinch of kelp
in the deep nook where

*one thing leads to another and a sort*
*of shape returns; not much, but still a way*

*of keeping in touch; absence remarking*
*presence, as somebody said, and*

the insect word – "Like this?"
– still noiseless, yes,
but much busier than
I'd thought.

        How the rain
in circles and circles
as if the echoes
of some voices who …
or maybe it's how one
other time when
the log that moved yesterday
is not moving and
slowly turning –

        like
when it's so hot and you can finally
take it off and just stand
in front of the mirror
and scratch –

or wait a little longer
and walk into the water.

        What
in me is clear, muddy and mix
till apt time of that
once over lightly
before the dark.

        The last poem
is very important.

It has always been necessary.

Now it is possible.

## Let These Bones Rejoice!

It may be and must be then – no;
a particle yet, untransformable
clings me, lazar and house
together – the first sin
is belief: grant me, old Fury, a scratch yet
of thy doubt – and when
you don't know all the words,
make 'em up, till whatever's left
(again) before each other start.

The scatter 'ems, tendrils,
tendons are they?
who? if never a naming
and whether the some of these,
my wordings here, and
hop to the rockside
of once their covering.

[check ms. for flood ref.]

Item: whatever happened to,
for instance, the raven?

My edges are getting edgy again.
What if I fall off?
(What if I don't?)

           Not yet
(at least I don't think so).

The "story," as they say, continuing,
and that awkward crow momently precise
as it enters my brain.

*Two men and a woman were cast away
on an island. After a while she grew
ashamed of what she was doing and killed*

*herself. After a while they grew ashamed*
*of what they were doing and buried her.*
*After a while they grew ashamed of what*
*they were doing and dug her up again.*

                    Was it you,
Old Murder, who warned me
there'd be ways like this? and always
something other, and always something less.

Item:
my new lover suggests
that I give my penis a name –
what about Poe?
whose white stuff
on the grass.

                    That
any conclusion, as the Stroller says,
can be deduced from a false premise.

And I am not afraid to die but
I am afraid to end the poem

# Beneath the Malebolge

*Beneath the Malebolge lies Hastings Street*
– Clarence Malcolm Lowry

Is this it, then? the story I've been trying to find
without knowing that it was lost, and the story
is the loss? The old farter shakes himself
a moment awake and wondering who or if
some other choices dying in the wilderness.

But not quite yet. I'll write that one later.
Some poems just don't know what day's good for them.
Another six hours or so should see it done,
I guess, or maybe something less than what
I watched the heron casually picking

and choosing, pays no particular attention
to who the sun jaggedly through this dust
approaching, large, redder each day, till splits,
the ambit still a little spongy where world
gulped, shifts, and the squinty apparent sky like a hand
through glass, whose gesture only knowable, repeating
a scattered count of precise, contentedly gleaming
blood drops left over on the palette, or
a circumstantial fossil brushed at wing tip
and something like what happened, happens again.

Was this his walking to? Not yet maybe, but
not much further either; the vague foreknowings
familiar now, and whatever else I could copy
a here of the loosely dust; that crinkle of light
at sedge-bitten the lake edge, and he reaches
and is seen reaching – himself or another –
into motionless the eddies of this once
and unencountered place? I don't remember.

& I remember, briefly and incoherently
yet with a fist enough flexible to trace
the scatter a thirtyfold of whatever mournings
two breaths away from meeting the greeter as
he breaks new eggs in *Salve!* to mutter across

these geomantic stones till – Pht! The old starter
still a little bit ahead of me, just around
the patiently rubbed corners unhoping till
under the malebolge, and a little south-
easted from Main and Hastings we lay us down to weep.

Follow me follow. That would have been in /54
or thereabouts – so we did a wrinkle between
the scratches, still sober (well, undrunk) enough to map
the gap of our hithers and thitherings, though
not quite able to remember next week even
if I have to wait
another 600 years or so when neither
of us may be interested any more, and blue
over blue until the last articulation
of these clouds after rain, as
if I said it more quietly this time and yet
a chance for who the me-thing boogeying back
the blackberry trail and finally I figured
he had no more blood in him.

                      But "Call me a Clarie,"
he slouched out the old Groucho line. He jams
half a pack of Sportsmans
into my pocket. "It's getting Juner again, so 'scuse
me a moment, please. I've got to totter off
and have another death."

                  He grinned and turned away
with a little twitch,
a dog shaking itself; and how a slurring
of rain containing his shadow, and then dry,
and nothing moving.

                         ∽

He takes a quick inventory of the relevant bits
and bones (Now I lay me downly), listens for a mo
to the sounds of one gull flying around the harbour
before the madness is complete.

                              He has nothing
in particular to say this morning,
pole and pebble equally
mute as a fruit (Let me finish),
frail as the Southern Cross, that oddly
embarrassed structure in the undulating night.

He goes for a walk because his pants are wet.
Even the crows have forgotten where he lives.

# Notes

2      epigraph: "History," from the collection *History*.

7      epigraph: *A Vision of the Last Judgement*.

8      *little death*: an image for sexual climax.

13     epigraph: "Sequence, Sometimes Metaphysical," from *The Far Field*.

16     *Kennst du das Land?* (Do you know that country?): from Wolf's setting of the *Italian Songbook*.
*kennst du es wohl?*: do you know it?
*Dahin*: There.
*wo die Zitronen blühn*: where the lemon trees bloom.

21     epigraph: *Troilus and Criseyde*.

23     *ana- / duomene*: foam-born, the traditional epithet applied to the goddess Aphrodite.

30     *blauen licht die Fernen*: the horizon becomes blue (i.e., blends with the sky), from Mahler's *Das Lied von der Erde*.

31     *alle Sehnsucht will nun träumen*: all longing will turn into dreaming, from *Das Lied von der Erde*.

32     *ohne Ruh, und suche Ruh*: without rest and seeking rest, from Schubert's song cycle *Die Winterreise (Winter Journey)*.

34     *de profundis clamavi ad te*: out of the depths I call to Thee, Psalm 130.

37     epigraph: *Paradise Lost*, Book X.

39     *Selah*: pause – a musical instruction found in the Book of Psalms.

42     *Enna*: the field in Sicily from which Persephone was captured by the god Hades and taken to the underworld.

51    *Kommos*: the last scene in a Greek tragedy, after the climax of the play; the recession of the surviving characters.

53    epigraph: "The Return," *Money and Rain*.

59    *La Corona*: My idea for this sequence came from John Donne's seven-part series of linked sonnets of the same title.
      *makeless*: matchless

69    epigraph: "Sequence, Sometimes Metaphysical."
      The theologian we know as Thomas à Kempis, author of *The Imitation of Christ*, was born Thomas Haemerken in the village of Kempen in the Netherlands. In 1392, at the age of twelve, Thomas walked to Deventer where he joined the monastic order of the Brothers of the Common Life.

73    *in cruce pro homine*: was crucified for mankind (the Creed).

75    epigraph: *Pierre*.

77    *Jantees* is my neologism, based on an obsolete form of "jaunt," to designate a kind of unexpected fellow traveller.

80    *blue man*: Odin, the Norse itinerant truth-seeker, is said to have always worn a blue cloak.

81    *resheph*: A burning coal, as in Isaiah's image for the fearful power of the prophetic message.

82    *pro ... ora ...*: reversed fragments of *ora pro nobis* (pray for us).

87    epigraph: from the sonnet "who's most afraid of death?" (*xli poems*).

88    *shaqed*: branch of an almond tree; an image of Jeremiah's call to prophecy.
      *Driftwood ... overhead*: from Capt. George Vancouver's *A Voyage of Discovery*, describing his exploration of the Pacific Northwest in 1798.
      *lotan*: Leviathan.

90    *I have a sinne of feare*: from Donne's "A Hymn to God the Father."
*the Stroller*: Aristotle (the Peripatetic).

91    *the Port-Royaliste*: Pascal. I am thinking here of his statement in the *Pensées*: "Le silence éternel de ces espaces infinis m'effraie" (the eternal silence of these infinite spaces terrifies me).

93    *that man*: Van Gogh.

94    *L'Invitation au voyage*: Baudelaire, in *Les Fleurs du Mal*.
*rhododactulos eos*: the rosy-fingered dawn, Homer's epithet from the Odyssey.
*The poet and his son*: Lawrence Ferlinghetti and Lorenzo travelled up the Northwest coast in 1978 (see *Northwest Ecolog*).

95    The American poet Stanley Cooperman lived for many years in Vancouver and Burnaby, B.C. Greco and Crazy Harry were among his many literary personae. Cooperman committed suicide in April, 1976.
Poet and teacher Pat Lowther was murdered at the age of 40 by her husband Roy in September, 1975.
Eric Ivan Berg, born in Quesnel, B.C., in 1948, was a poet, disc jockey, and film-maker. He died in a logging accident in August, 1977.

99    epigraph: the first line of "Christ Walks in this Infernal District too" (*Selected Poems*, ed. Earle Birney).
*Malebolge*: the "ditch of evil" that forms the eighth circle of Dante's *Inferno*.

# Acknowledgements

*The Almond Tree* (Quarry Press, 1985), *Antics Against the Long Night* (Far Field Press, 1998), *The Burden of Jonah ben Amittai* (Quarry Press, 1991), *Forgetting* (Nebula Press, 1992), *Imagines* (Leaf Press, 2002), *Locatives* (Nebula Press, 1982), *Poetry Canada Review* Vol. 15, No. 2 (1995), *This Stranger Wood* (Quarry Press, 1982), *Winter Journey* (Quarry Press, 1984).

Thanks to Allan Briesmaster for his sensitive and sympathetic understanding of my intentions with this selection; to A. F. Moritz for his meticulous attention to details and his firm yet flexible grasp of the whole; and to Russell Thornton for his enthusiastic and continuous support for the project.

# About the Author

Allan Brown was born in Victoria and presently lives in Powell River, BC. His poems have been published in various Canadian journals since 1962, and partly collected in sixteen books and chapbooks, and in several anthologies. He was writer-in-residence at the Kapuskasing Public Library 1987-88. His collection *Imagines* (Leaf Press, 2002) was co-winner of the bp Nichol Chapbook Award.

His critical writings – mostly reviews and review articles – have appeared since 1976. He was guest editor for *Nebula* 1979-80, literary editor of *Quarry* 1982-84 and guest editor in 1986, and a member of the editorial board of *Rim* 1998-99. He has been the contributing editor for reviews to *Jones Av.* since 1996, and has edited and published *The Wayward Coast* anthology series since 2001.

He is a member of the Canadian Poetry Association, the Federation of BC Writers, Haiku Canada, the League of Canadian Poets, the pacifi-kana haiku group, and is artistic director of the Malaspina Writers' Association.